Sports Stars

ALAN TRAMMELL

Tiger On The Prowl

By Barry Janoff

CHILDRENS PRESS ™

CHICAGO

Cover photograph: G. Robarge
Inside photographs courtesy of the following:
Allen M. Einstein, pages 6, 12, 15, 17, 20, 24, 38, 41,
and 43
Mike Valeri, pages 9 and 18
G. Robarge, pages 22, 28, and 34
Nancy Hogue, page 30

Library of Congress Cataloging in Publication Data

Janoff, Barry.
    Alan Trammell: tiger on the prowl.

    (Sports stars)
    Summary: A brief biography highlighting the career of the
star shortstop of the Detroit Tigers baseball team.
    1. Trammell, Alan, 1958-   —Juvenile literature.
2. Baseball players—United States—Biography—Juvenile
literature. 3. Detroit Tigers (Baseball team)—Juvenile
literature. [1. Trammell, Alan, 1958-   . 2. Baseball players.]
I. Title. II. Series.
GV865.T68J36 1985   796.357'092'4 [B] [92] 84-28490
ISBN 0-516-04342-0

    2 3 4 5 6 7 8 9 10 R 94 93 92 91 90 89 88 87 86

Sports Stars

ALAN TRAMMELL

Tiger On The Prowl

When he was a young boy, Alan Trammell had a dream. More than anything else, he wanted to play baseball.

Today, Alan Trammell plays shortstop for the Detroit Tigers. He is one of the best players in baseball.

"When you work hard," says Alan, "you can make your dreams come true."

In 1984 the Detroit Tigers had one of their best seasons ever. A big reason they did so well was because Alan was an important part of the team. He can hit. He plays his position without making mistakes. And he is a leader who always helps his teammates.

"Without Alan, we would not be as good as we are," says his manager, Sparky Anderson. "Alan is a key member of this team."

Trammell has come a long way to reach his dream. After the 1983 season he hurt his knee. Some people thought he would never play again.

The injury happened on Halloween. Alan was at a party dressed as the monster Frankenstein. He tripped and fell. Then he heard a "pop" in his knee. One month later he had to have surgery. The doctors thought it might be a long time before his knee was back to normal.

But Alan is a fighter. He worked hard and got his knee into shape. When the season started Alan was playing shortstop. He was stronger and faster than ever.

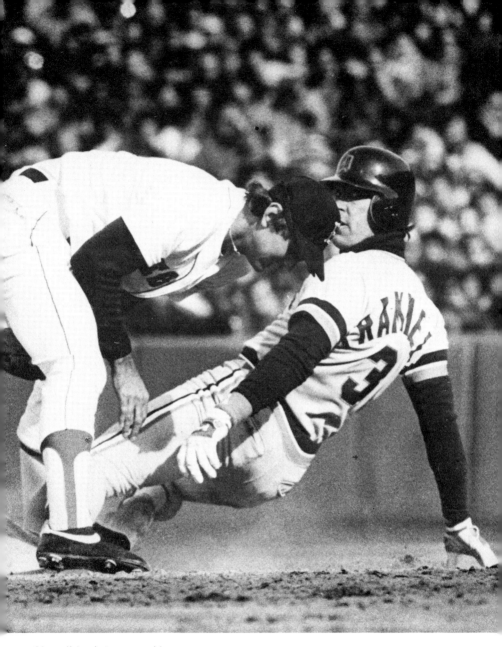

Alan slides into second base

That was not the first time Alan had to work hard to solve a problem.

"In 1982 I was in a batting slump. I was unsure of myself. My batting average was only .206 in the middle of the season.

"I knew I needed help. So I went to the Tigers' batting coach, Gates Brown. Brown used to be a star with the Tigers. He knew a lot about hitting."

Brown and Trammell worked together. Alan put in many long hours trying to improve. Many times he stayed after the games were over to practice his hitting. When it was dark outside, he would go to a room deep inside Tiger Stadium to practice his swing.

The hard work paid off. Alan hit more than .300 for the rest of the season. The next season, 1983, he finished with a .319 average. That was his best batting average ever.

In 1984, his average was .314. That was the sixth-best average in the American League and the best average on his team. He also won the Golden Glove Award, which is given to the player who is the best at his position on the field. That was the fourth time that Alan had won the Golden Glove Award.

In 1983 Alan also had 30 stolen bases. That was more stolen bases than any Tiger shortstop had had in one season since 1917! For Alan, working hard means being a complete player.

When Alan is on base, the opposing team must watch him very carefully. Alan is very good at stealing bases.

"When I was hitting .200 in 1982, things were looking down," remembers Alan. "I wasn't handling it very well. I couldn't get out of the bad groove. I was getting mad and frustrated with myself.

"But then I realized that I was trying to do too many things at one time. I realized that I had to correct my problems one step at a time. That was the biggest point in my career, right there. I could have been buried if I hadn't come out of my slump.

"The team stuck with me," adds Alan. "I fought out of the slump. It made me a better ballplayer."

Alan was born in Garden Grove, California, in 1958. Garden Grove is a suburb of San Diego. Alan remembers spending a lot of time at the baseball stadium watching games. He also spent a lot of time trying to meet the players to get their autographs and their old bats:

"I got to be a pain," Alan says. "But I had a lot of energy."

Today, Alan remembers those days and signs autographs for any fan who asks for one.

It was as a young boy that Alan knew he had baseball in his blood. From the time he saw his first game, he knew that his goal was to become a big league ball player.

Alan poses with the movie actor Roy Scheider, the star of "2010" and "Tiger Town."

"People ask me, 'What would you do if you hadn't made it in baseball?' " Alan explains. "I don't know. Playing baseball is the only thing I ever really wanted to do."

In public school Alan worked hard at his studies. As a reward his teachers helped him to follow his dream of becoming a baseball player. When he was 10 years old, Alan's school in San Diego set up a program that allowed one student in each class to watch the World Series on television during school hours.

"Because I had worked so hard in class, I was picked as the one in my class to watch. This was in 1968. The funny thing was that one of the teams in the World Series was the Detroit Tigers." Alan watched the Tigers beat the St. Louis Cardinals in an exciting World Series.

Newscasters always ask Alan what he would do if he didn't play baseball.

Now, Alan plays for the Tigers. He knows that kids across the country are watching him on television.

"I remember watching the players on television," says Alan. "Something was extra-special because it was the World Series. I said to myself, 'I want to play in the World Series.' Being there means that your team is the very best."

In 1984 Alan saw his dream come true. The Detroit Tigers won the World Series, beating the San Diego Padres, four games to one. Alan says that winning the World Series was, "the greatest thrill in my baseball career."

Steve Garvey, first baseman for the San Diego Padres, waits for a throw from the pitcher to keep Alan on base.

When he was older, Alan went to Kearny High School. In high school he played baseball and basketball. He was so good that he was named to the California Interscholastic Team in both sports. That meant that he was one of the best high school athletes in the whole state!

In June, 1976, Alan was picked by the Tigers on the second round of the amateur draft. Two days after he graduated from high school he was playing in the minor leagues. His first team was the Bristol Tigers. This team was for players in their first year of professional baseball.

Alan was one of the best players in the league that season. He batted .271. He was named to the All-Star team. Alan was so good that he moved to the Montgomery Rebels. This team was just two levels below playing in the major leagues. Many players need two or three years to reach that level. But Alan had done it in less than one year.

The next season, 1977, was a big one for Alan. He played 134 games for Montgomery. He batted .291. He had 50 runs batted in and had 19 triples, which was the best in the league. Because he worked so hard, Alan was named the most valuable player (MVP) in the league. That meant he did more to help his team than any other player had done to help their team that season.

Alan and his teammates are happy that they won the World Series.

"Being named MVP was important to me," says Alan. "It meant that I had done my job. It also meant that the team had done well. In baseball, you play for a team. That means that everything you do should help the team.

"When I won the MVP award, I told my teammates and coaches that the award was for everyone. It had my name on it, but the honor was something that I wanted to share with everyone on the team."

In 1984 Alan shared another honor with his team. In the World Series he batted .450, which was the best average among the players on Detroit and San Diego. He also had two home runs and six runs batted in. Because he played so well, Alan was named MVP of the World Series. "This is the highlight," Alan smiled. "We get the World Series ring and they can't take that away from us."

In 1976 and 1977 his team at Montgomery won the championship of the league. That meant that they were the very best. Alan then wanted to do the same thing for the Tigers. He wanted them to be the very best.

Alan was still a teenager. But he was so good that the Tigers moved him into the major leagues that season. In 1977 he played 19 games for the Tigers. He never played in the minor leagues again.

When coaches and players talk about Alan Trammell, the word they use most is "consistent." They like the way he plays every day. Even when he is in a slump, he tries his best.

"I always liked him," says Whitey Herzog, manager of the St. Louis Cardinals. "I always thought Alan was as good on defense as anybody I had ever seen."

"He comes out and plays tough every game," adds Yogi Berra, manager of the New York Yankees. "He is consistent. He tries to do something in every game that will help his team win."

Alan says that being consistent is something he learned as a kid. His parents taught him good habits at home. In school he knew that good work habits would help him to become a better student. And on the ball field he knew that good

work habits would help him to become a better athlete.

"I've always been told, 'The way you practice is the way you play,'" says Alan. "Some players get lazy during practice. They'll pick up a ground ball with one hand instead of two. Or they'll fool around and not throw the ball the way they should."

What Alan does is to pretend that every practice is a real game. That way, he will be better prepared when the real game starts.

"In practice I try to get in front of every ground ball," Alan continues. "I catch every ball with two hands, like I do in a game. I try to be consistent. That's the whole thing."

As Mike Hargrove of the Cleveland Indians slides into base, Alan tries to get out of his way.

Alan says that he watched many players while he was growing up. But two players that he watched the closest were Mark Belanger and Eddie Brinkman. Both were shortstops in the major leagues. Both were considered to be among the best at their position.

"They both got in front of every ball," says Alan. "They tried to throw accurately. They were consistent."

Alan takes baseball very seriously. But he also has a lot of fun. He enjoys playing and has a love for the game.

"If I didn't enjoy what I was doing," he says, "I would not be as good as I am."

Part of his fun comes off the field. Teammates saw that Alan was a messy eater at mealtime. When they all sat down to have lunch or dinner, a lot of Alan's food ended up on the floor or on his shirt. One teammate called him, "The World's Worst Eater." Another teammate wondered if any food ever reached Alan's stomach because so much was on the table and floor.

Alan, who is six feet tall and weighs 175 pounds, cannot explain why his eating habits are messy. He only smiles and says, "I was always a messy eater. Even as a kid. When I eat, I drop things."

Alan laughs when he says, "When I'm playing in a ball game, I don't drop anything. Maybe I should eat my meals at second base."

In 1978 Alan's hard work made him an important part of the Tigers. He was only 20 years old, but he had become the team's best shortstop. He played in 139 games and batted .268. On the field he and second baseman Lou Whitaker, another of Detroit's young stars, helped the Tigers to record 177 double plays. That total was the best figure in the American League.

Alan was named one of baseball's best rookies that season. But he had other reasons to be happy. Before the season started, Alan married Barbara Leverett, a girl he had known since high school. They were married on February 21, which also is Alan's birthday.

When Alan was in a batting slump, his family and teammates
supported him.

Today, Alan and Barbara have two sons, Kyle and Lance. Lance was named after Lance Parrish, who is the star catcher for the Tigers.

"I won't push them," says Alan of his sons. "But if they want to become baseball players, I will support them all the way."

Alan has had a lot of support in his career from family and teammates. When he was in a batting slump in 1982, his coaches and teammates supported him. They gave him the strength to improve.

When he had knee surgery before the 1984 season, his family gave him the support he needed. His knee was in a brace for seven weeks. Then he spent two more months getting his knee back in shape for the baseball season.

"My family and friends were very helpful to me," Alan recalls. "I had to spend a lot of time getting my knee strong again. I had to work harder than ever. I never had had an injury like that before. I was scared."

The support of his family and friends worked. His knee became stronger and stronger. When the season started, he was ready to play.

The Tigers won their opening game and looked like winners. After 40 games they had lost only five times! The Tigers were in first place for the entire season. Alan's hitting and strong fielding were key reason's for Detroit's super season.

Some people were surprised that Alan Trammell was such an important part of the team.

But people who watch baseball were not surprised. Alan's progress has been steady during his career. Even when he did not hit well in 1981 and 1982, he was able to do things that other players couldn't do. He always was able to find a way to help his team win.

In 1979 Alan improved in many areas from his rookie season of 1978. His batting average went up to .276. His total number of hits went up to 127, and he had 17 stolen bases. He was becoming a faster player, too.

In 1980 Alan improved even more. He batted .300 for the first time in his professional career. He scored 107 runs—one of the top totals in the whole league. The total also was one of the best in the history of the Tigers.

That season the Tigers proved to Alan that they wanted to keep him on the team for a long time. Alan signed a seven-year contract with

All the fans of the Tigers really celebrated when they won the World Series in 1984.

the team. It was worth almost three million dollars.

Soon, the contract was extended for two more years. Trammell now has a contract with the Tigers that will last into 1989. And he expects to be with the team for years after that, until he retires.

"If any player on our club deserves that kind of money, he does," said Jim Campbell, the general manager of the Tigers.

"When they offered me the contract, I jumped at it," says Alan. "How many people can get a seven-year contract for good money? And guaranteed? If I get hurt, I still get paid!"

Some players who sign big contracts do not seem to work as hard as they should. But Alan worked even harder. The money was important to him. But something else was more important. "Security," he says. "With that, I'm a happy person."

Alan's hitting totals were down in 1981 and 1982. But he became better than ever on the field. And he worked to improve his batting average. Fans and people in baseball were impressed.

"The oldtimers will be mad at me for saying this, but there are three shortstops in this league who are probably as good as any who have ever played the game," says Dick Howser, manager of the Kansas City Royals. Howser used to play second base in the major leagues. He has seen many players, good and bad.

Alan is one of the best shortstops in baseball today.

"Those three players are Robin Yount, Cal Ripken Jr., and Alan Trammell."

Yount plays shortstop for the Milwaukee Brewers. In 1982 he was the most valuable player in the American League.

Ripken plays shortstop for the Baltimore Orioles. In 1983 he was the most valuable player in the American League.

Howser and others feel that Alan Trammell is at least as good as Yount and Ripken.

"If he doesn't get hurt, Trammell has a chance to be one of the greatest ever to play shortstop," Howser says.

Alan's manager, Sparky Anderson adds, "I don't think that baseball has ever seen three shortstops who every year will be in the top 10 in the MVP voting, the way it is now."

Alan Trammell has had much success. But he has not changed much from the young boy who once hung out at San Diego Stadium. He still loves to play baseball. He still has a lot of energy. He still works hard to be the best player he can and to make his team the best.

And he is still a messy eater.

What will he do in the future? He is only in his late twenties. He says he can play until he is 35 or 36. At that age, he could retire as one of the greatest shortstops ever.

Many feel that he is one of the greatest short-stops of all time right now.

"The important thing is that you set a goal and work toward that goal," he says. "If you have limitations, you have to know what they are. I know I'm not going to hit 30 home runs a season. But I can hit 10 or 15 a season. And that's good enough.

"My strengths are in other areas—getting singles and doubles, playing in the field without making mistakes, and working for my team and for my teammates. But most of all, by being the best person I can, on and off the field."

With his career on the rise and his family life better than ever, Alan has many reasons to be happy with his life. But is there anything he would change, if he could?

"I wouldn't trade it," he smiles. "I wouldn't change a thing."

CHRONOLOGY

1958—Alan Stuart Trammell is born on February 21 in Garden Grove, California.

1968—Alan watches the Detroit Tigers win the World Series.

1976—Alan graduates from Kearny High School and is drafted by the Detroit Tigers.
He joins the Bristol Tigers and is named to the All-Star Team.

1977—Alan hits .291 with 50 RBIs for Montgomery and is named MVP of the Southern League. His team wins the league championship.
He is called up to the Detroit Tigers in September.

1978—Alan marries his high school sweetheart, Barbara Leverett.
He hits .268 for the Tigers and is named to *Baseball Digest* magazine's All-Rookie team.

1980—Alan signs a seven-year contract for $2.8 million.
He hits .300 for the first time in his professional career.

1982—Alan suffers through a batting slump in the first half of the season, but battles back to have a superb second half.

1983—Alan hits .319, the best average in his career, and fourth best in the American League.
He suffers an off-season knee injury that requires surgery.

1984—Alan recovers from knee injury and hits .314. He leads Detroit to victory in the World Series against the San Diego Padres. Alan hits .450 with six RBIs and two home runs and is named MVP of the World Series.

1985—The Tigers did not have a very good season and Alan's average was only .258. But American and National managers voted Alan one of the 3 smartest players in the major leagues.

ABOUT THE AUTHOR

Barry Janoff has been writing about sports for more than 10 years. He has covered professional, college, and high school sports for numerous sports publications and has interviewed many of the top athletes in America. In 1982 he spent three weeks touring Yugoslavia with the U.S. Women's Olympic Basketball Team, many of whom were on the Gold Medal squad in the 1984 Olympics. His work has appeared in *HOOP*, the official magazine of the National Basketball Association; *KICK*, the magazine of the North American Soccer League; *Football Digest*, *Basketball Digest*, and *Soccer Digest*; CBS Publications; and the Associated Features series of sports books. For the past two years he has been Sports Editor for Laurant Publications, which prints a variety of national sports and entertainment magazines and books.

$$1\atop38$$
38
——
76

$$2\atop76$$

24

$$30\ 4$$
152
——
18 24

36
2
——